Marie's Magnificent Recipes

Cooking Well

by

Joyce Marie Ross

authorHOUSE®

AuthorHouse™
1663 Liberty Drive, Suite 200
Bloomington, IN 47403
www.authorhouse.com
Phone: 1-800-839-8640

First published by AuthorHouse 3/9/2009

ISBN: 978-1-4033-7691-6 (e)
ISBN: 978-1-4033-7692-3 (sc)

Printed in the United States of America
Bloomington, Indiana

This book is printed on acid-free paper.

Contents

A NOTE FROM THE AUTHOR

Dear Reader,

I am very happy to be able to share these recipes with you, which are my own inventions that family and friends have enjoyed for years.

My name is Joyce Marie Ross. Growing up in Selma, Alabama, I became aware at an early age of my special gift for inventing recipes. When I was a young teenager, I used to cook cornbread for my family that was warm and moist on the inside and crispy and brown on the outside, and no one could get enough of it. But I invented most of the recipes in this book for my husband, Charles Edward Ross, who really loved my cookies, especially the Cherry Almond Delights, which I am now preparing to sell commercially. I used to just go into the kitchen and start experimenting by combining different ingredients and cooking them in different ways.

Even though the recipes in this book are truly my own, many of them were inspired by my great aunt, Auntie Alberta, who I used to help bake meals and desserts for weddings and other events at church. As I say at the end of this book, her egg custard pie just made me melt! I soon started cooking and baking on my own for the R.I.C.A. class at my church, Queen of Peace Roman Catholic Church in Selma, and also for my cosmetology class, and they liked my recipes so much that they starting spreading the word around town. Before I knew it, I was baking large batches of Cherry Almond Delights for the Our House restaurant in Selma with the help of my old friend Bernice Gill who let me use her kitchen in West Selma, and Ms. Joyce Rutledge, a professional cook. When my friends at Alabama State University in Montgomery tried some of my recipes they encouraged me to start working with the Small Business Center there, where I came up with a plan for marketing my recipes and cookies. I expect to be selling some of them commercially in the near future, but I'd love to have you try them for yourselves!

My, my, my, what a blessing Auntie Alberta has been in my life! I said to myself that one day I would bake and cook like her, and that has always been my goal. I hope you find the new line of recipes in this book as tasty and delicious as my family and friends have done. No one but me, to my knowledge, has ever come up with these Blasting Recipe Inventions, so please take them into your kitchens and start enjoying them! And let me know how you like them!

I want to give special thanks to Ms. Joyce Rutledge, the professional cook who helped me in Selma, and my friend Bernice Gill in West Selma who let me use her kitchen, and also my friends at Queen of Peace Roman Catholic Church in Selma and my other friends and family members who gave me so much encouragement and support, including Mr. Michael Dixon, who has helped me financially from time to time, and my English teacher from cosmetology school in Selma, who helped me with my writing. Wally Amos, who invented the Famous Amos Cookie line, has also given me a lot of good business advice and encouragement, as have my friends at the Small Business Center of Alabama State University in Montgomery, and my attorney, Mr. James Arndt. My heartfelt thanks to all of you for making this book possible!

Joyce Marie Ross
Evanston, Illinois
June, 2008

CHICKEN CHERRY SANDWICH

This recipe is for family of four.

4 Chicken Breast
1 Tablespoon of salt
1 tablespoon of black pepper
1 onion
2 cups of flour
1 ½ cup of milk
½ cup of Crisco
½ teaspoon Jalapeno peppers
1/3 cup of cherries (chopped)

Directions:

First boil chicken with a tablespoon of salt, a tablespoon of black pepper and one whole onion in a boiler for 15 minutes. Take chicken from boiler and chop it up finely. Next, make up dough using self-rising flour, milk, and Crisco oil. Knead the dough. Roll dough out and cut round. Next, add the chicken, cherries, and peppers in center of the dough. Fold dough over like a sandwich then press around the sides sealing the dough. Now, place in oven at 325⁰ for 30 minutes or until medium brown.

NOTES

NOTES

NOTES

NOTES

NOTES

MARIE'S PAW GLAZE

2 cups of coconut milk
6 packages of Sweet-N-Low sugar
3 egg whites
1/3 cup of butter
1 teaspoon of flour
¼ teaspoon of pure vanilla flavor

<u>Directions:</u>

Mix coconut milk, egg whites, flavor, and melted butter. Pour all dry ingredients with liquid ingredients and mix for 1 ½ to 2 minutes. Serve on Cakes or Doughnuts.

NOTES

NOTES

NOTES

NOTES

NOTES

MINIT CHICKEN BATTER SANDWICH

1 tablespoon of salt
6 chicken breasts
4 jalapeno peppers
¼ cup of honey
4 cups of flour
1 ½ cup of cashews
3 tablespoons of cinnamon
1 cup of parsley
1 ½ cup of lemon pepper

Directions:

Mix honey, jalapeno peppers, lemon pepper and salt in pot. Boil chicken breasts for 45 minutes. Next, drain and keep chicken broth. Mix flour into a dough, roll dough out, and then place ¼ cup of all ingredients, cashew nuts, cinnamon, and a teaspoon of parsley into the center of every sandwich. Roll dough over two to three times. Final step: bake in oven at 325⁰ for 11 to 12 minutes.

NOTES

NOTES

NOTES

NOTES

NOTES

SALTAE BLACKEYE PEAS FRIED

<u>Serves a family of eight:</u>

1 bag of black-eye peas
3 whole jalapeno peppers
2 cups of soy sauce
8 cups of water
1 teaspoon of black pepper
1 teaspoon of salt
2 ½ cups of cooking sherry
1 cup of cottage cheese
1 cup of pineapples

<u>Directions:</u>

Cook the black-eye peas for 1hour and 40 minutes. When done drain from liquid. Put in cooking sherry for 6 minutes. Next take from sherry. Next use oil and frying pan and fry for 15 minutes. When done top it off with cottage cheese and pineapples.

NOTES

NOTES

NOTES

NOTES

NOTES

JOY VEGETABLE AND MEAT ROLL

½ Cabbage
1 cup of spinach
1 cup of pink salmon
½ apple
½ cup of parsley
1 tablespoon of Lawry's seasoning sauce
1 cup of ground beef
1 ½ cup of flour
¼ teaspoon of butter

Directions:

Boil cabbage for 30 minutes. Next mix dough ¼ teaspoon of butter in with dough batter. Next take all ingredients above place in center. Then roll the dough over three times. Next pull in sides of dough. Next baked on 325^0 for 30 minutes for a nine-inch roll. When done take out of oven and cut in half.

NOTES

NOTES

NOTES

NOTES

NOTES

GREEN EGGS AND HAM

6 slices of Pits ham
12 eggs
1 cup of almonds
½ box of raisins
1 cup of honey
1 whole onion cut
1 teaspoon of green food coloring

Direction:

Mix in bowl, green food coloring, almonds, onion, and eggs for 1 minute. Pour into frying pan for best results use Crisco oil. Next, take a slice of pits ham and fry in Crisco oil until done. After frying ham pour honey and raisins on top and then serve.

NOTES

NOTES

NOTES

NOTES

NOTES

DESSERT NUT AND FRUIT CANDY

¼ cup of Hershey cocoa
¼ cup of strawberries
¼ cup of cashew nuts
¼ cup of Karo syrup
1 cup dry coconut
1 cup pecan

Directions:

Use dessert glass to prepare and serve. First put in Hershey cocoa, strawberries, cashew nuts, kayo syrup, dry coconut, and pecan; then serve.

NOTES

NOTES

NOTES

NOTES

NOTES

BANANA-DO-LA

2   Cups flour
1/3 Teaspoon salt
¼   Cup Crisco oil
4   Bananas
1 1/3 Cups milk
½   Cup cinnamon
1 ½ Cups sugar
1   Teaspoon vanilla flavor or extract
1   Teaspoon baking powder

<u>Directions:</u>

Mix flour, sugar and baking powder together. Then mix the Crisco, vanilla flavor and milk, and pour all ingredients (except bananas and cinnamon) into one bowl and mix until thick. Knead and then slice the dough into pencil sizes, then roll the dough into a twist, and sprinkle the dough with cinnamon. Next, with a spatula, wipe the crushed bananas on top of the twisted dough. Bake at 350 degrees for a half hour or until crispy and brown.

NOTES

NOTES

NOTES

NOTES

NOTES

BULLSEYE FISH

1 cup of parsley
1 tablespoon of dry garlic
1 green pepper
1 green bell pepper
2 cups of flour
1 teaspoon of lemon pepper
1 tablespoon of basil
1 jalapeno pepper
1 whole eggplant
1 cup of plain peanuts
1 cup of karo syrup

Directions:

Mix Lemon pepper, flour, basil, green pepper, jalapeno pepper, green bell pepper, garlic. Next, put fish in batter. Fry fish until golden brown. Then cut the center of fish open. Stuff the fish with parsley, peanuts, cooked eggplant, and a little cornbread dressing. Then seal with karo syrup. It's now ready to serve.

NOTES

NOTES

NOTES

NOTES

NOTES

ALMOND FISH

<u>Serves a family of six:</u>

6 pieces of fish
1 ½ cup of meal
1 cup of chopped almonds
4 eggs
¼ cup of karo syrup
1 red hot pepper
1 green hot pepper
1 tablespoon tartar sauce

<u>Directions:</u>

Mix eggs, karo syrup, and sliced almonds in a bowl for 30 seconds. Next, take one piece of fish at a time and dip into mixture. Take each piece of fish and batter in meal. Bake fish in oven until golden brown at 350^0. Then garnish the fish with red and green hot peppers. Now top it off with a tablespoon of tartar sauce and serve.

NOTES

NOTES

NOTES

NOTES

NOTES

CABBAGE LEAF SAFARI

1   Head of cabbage
1   Package of roast beef
4   Avocados
1   Package cream cheese
4   Mangoes

<u>Directions:</u>

Boil cabbage 25 minutes. Boil roast beef 1 hour 15 minutes. Peel avocados and mangoes, and slice them up. Slice meat into small chunks and put onto single leaves of cabbage. Add avocados to the leaves and spread 1/3 cup of mango chunks. Roll up the cabbage leaves and hold them together with toothpicks. Bake at 350 degrees for 30 minutes until well done. Spread the cream cheese on top of the cabbage rolls and eat.

NOTES

NOTES

NOTES

NOTES

NOTES

CORNBREAD

2 cups self-rising corn meal
¼ cup Crisco Oil
2 Eggs
4-5 tablespoons self-rising flour
Vitamin D Milk
1/3 cup of sugar
1 cup cracklin' pork chips/pork rinds

Directions:

Mix corn meal, eggs, sugar, flour and broken-up cracklin' pork chips into a bowl and add melted Crisco oil. Next pour in the milk as needed for a thick batter. Stir 20 strokes and pour into a greased cornbread pan. Then insert the pan into the oven and bake at 350 degrees until crispy and brown. Serve.

NOTES

NOTES

NOTES

NOTES

NOTES

LAMB SALAD

1   Pound of lamb
2-3 Jars of horseradish mustard
5   Large Idaho Potatoes
5 or 6 Squashes
3   Fresh tomatoes
½   Bag Brussels sprouts

<u>Directions:</u>

Boil lamb for 2½ to 3 hours or until done but not falling apart. Boil squash and Brussels sprouts together, but don't overcook. Boil potatoes for 25 minutes. After boiling all ingredients, slice up the tomatoes, and pour all ingredients into a salad bowl. Mix the horseradish mustard into the ingredients, and serve.

NOTES

NOTES

NOTES

NOTES

NOTES

MARINATED STEAK YUM!

4   Slices of steak
2   Jalapeno peppers
1   Cup of strawberries
½   Cup of mayonnaise
2   Avocados

Directions:

Slice jalapeno peppers and strawberries, and add ½ cup of mayonnaise. Peel and slice the avocados. Put all ingredients into a blender and mix for five seconds. Cover the bottom of a large, flat baking pan with aluminum foil, pour the ingredients into the pan, and add the steak slices. Cover the pan with aluminum foil and let the steak marinate with the ingredients in the refrigerator for three hours. Take the pan from the refrigerator and sprinkle 3-4 tablespoons of flour over the ingredients. Then cover with foil, add water if needed. Bake at 350 degrees for two hours. Serve.

NOTES

NOTES

NOTES

NOTES

NOTES

PORK STEW POT

1   Pork shoulder
1   Tablespoon black pepper
2   Cans stewed tomatoes
2   Cups eggplant
1 ½ Cups kernel corn
1   Tablespoon Ms. Dash
2 ½ Cups Brussels sprouts
3   Cans tomato paste
2   Cups mushrooms
1   Tablespoon salt

<u>Directions:</u>

Cook pork shoulder in a large pot with ingredients. Mix all ingredients in this order. Be sure to use a big pot for the stew. Add water as needed. Simmer on stove for 2 ½ to 3 hours.

NOTES

NOTES

NOTES

NOTES

NOTES

ABOUT THE AUTHOR

I would like a moment of your time to introduce myself. I'm Joyce M. Ross, a forty-three year old woman. I grew up in Selma, Alabama. I became interested in cooking the moment I realized that I had discovered something special.

I came up with these recipes with inspiration from an old Great Aunt, Auntee Alberta. I believe she was the best baker in the world. Lord, the way she would make egg custard pie; when I was a child, it made me melt. Auntee Alberta was from Wilcox County, Alabama. My ex-husband, Mr. Charles Ross, loved sweets also. So one day while in the kitchen, I made a discovery of Marie's Magnificent Recipes.

My friends have given me good feedback from my cooking. My neighbors from Martin L. King Street like my cooking. Friends from my church R.C.I.A. class liked my cooking. My classmates in cosmetology liked my cooking.

My father as well as my mother, Johnny Lee McWilliams and Lola Bell McWilliams, inspired me to cook. I learned more about cooking in marriage. I have a friend whose name is Joyce Rutledge. She is a professional licensed cook. She also is an inspirational monument. One day while in the kitchen craving for something sweet, I made more discoveries, which I've included in this book.

My paternal Grandmother, Mary Frances McWilliams and maternal Grandmother, Rosa Bell Hines, were other good cooks in my family. Grandmother Mary cooked the best blackberry slickem dumplings. Grandmother Rosa cooked the best gingerbread in the world. My father taught me how to cook good fresh snap beans.

The best time to prepare Cherry Almond Delight Cookies, Sweet Hull Fruit Pie, Chicken Cherry Sandwich, and Marie Paw Glaze would be during the summer. Chicken batter, Almond Fish, Saltae Black-eye Peas Fried, Joy Vegetable and Meat Roll, and Dessert Nut and Fruit Candy are all made year round. Bulls Eye Fish is best prepared during June and July.

In conclusion, I would like to hope that someone would be fed. In the near future, I'm hoping to make one more invention in cooking; then I'll call it quits. I hope my first book will be a blessing from God.

My recipes are distinguished from others because they are new and have not been passed down from family and friends.